MENTAL HEALTH DIET COOKBOOK

Dr. Kimberly Carlos

Copyright © 2023 by Dr. Kimberly Carlos

TABLE OF CONTENT

INTRODUCTION

Once upon a time in a quiet, sun-dappled village nestled between rolling hills, there lived a woman named Emily. For as long as she could remember, Emily had battled with the shadows that plagued her mind – anxiety and depression. Every day was a relentless struggle against the darkness within, until she stumbled upon an unexpected source of hope.

Emily had always been a food enthusiast, and her curiosity led her down a different culinary path. She began to explore the world of nutrition and its impact on mental health. Armed with determination and a passion to heal herself, Emily embarked on a journey of self-discovery through her diet.

She started with small changes, replacing processed foods with fresh fruits, vegetables, and whole grains. Slowly but surely, Emily noticed a shift within herself. Her energy levels increased, and the heaviness in her chest began to dissipate. She felt more vibrant and alive with each passing day.

As her knowledge grew, so did her culinary skills. Emily discovered the power of foods rich in omega-3 fatty acids like salmon and flaxseeds, which eased her anxiety. She learned about the mood-boosting properties of dark chocolate and the calming effects of herbal teas like chamomile and lavender.

Emily's journey wasn't without challenges. She faced doubts, setbacks, and moments of weakness, but her determination carried her through. She also sought guidance from a nutritionist and a therapist, who provided invaluable support on her path to recovery.

Months turned into years, and Emily's transformation was nothing short of remarkable. Her once-constant companions, anxiety and depression, had retreated to the shadows. She had discovered a newfound sense of balance and clarity in her life.

Word of Emily's remarkable journey spread throughout the village, and she became a beacon of hope for others who suffered in silence.

She started a small support group where people could share their struggles and learn about the healing power of nutrition.

Together, they explored recipes and shared stories of progress. Emily's story became an inspiring testament to the connection between a healthy diet and mental well-being.

She had not only cured herself of the shadows that had haunted her but had also illuminated a path to healing for countless others.

 In her village, the transformative power of food on mental health had found a champion in Emily, proving that sometimes, the key to healing is as close as your own kitchen.

CHAPTER ONE

Following a Mental Health Diet with Benefits

Following a mental health diet can have numerous benefits for your emotional well-being and overall mental health. Here are some steps to help you adopt a diet that supports your mental well-being:

1. Consult a Healthcare Professional: Before making any significant changes to your diet, consult with a healthcare professional, such as a registered dietitian or a mental health expert. They can help you create a personalized plan that suits your specific needs and ensures you're getting all the essential nutrients.

2. Emphasize Whole Foods: Base your diet on whole, unprocessed foods like fruits, vegetables, whole grains, lean proteins, nuts, and seeds. These foods provide essential vitamins, minerals, and antioxidants that support brain health.

3. Include Omega-3 Fatty Acids: Omega-3 fatty acids, found in fatty fish like salmon, mackerel, and walnuts, have been associated with improved mood and reduced symptoms of depression. Aim to incorporate these foods into your diet regularly.

4. Choose Complex Carbohydrates: Complex carbohydrates like whole grains (brown rice, quinoa, whole wheat), legumes, and starchy vegetables can help stabilize blood sugar levels and provide a steady source of energy for your brain.

5. Prioritize Lean Proteins: Lean protein sources like poultry, lean beef, tofu, and beans contain amino acids that are important for neurotransmitter production. These neurotransmitters, like serotonin and dopamine, play a role in regulating mood.

6. Limit Sugar and Processed Foods: High sugar intake and processed foods can lead to energy crashes and mood swings. Reduce your consumption of sugary snacks, sodas, and highly processed foods.

7. Stay Hydrated: Dehydration can affect your mood and cognitive function. Drink plenty of water throughout the day to stay properly hydrated.

8. Moderate Caffeine and Alcohol: Excessive caffeine and alcohol intake can disrupt sleep and contribute to anxiety and depression. Limit your consumption and be mindful of how these substances affect your mental state.

9. Include Mood-Boosting Foods: Incorporate foods known for their mood-enhancing properties, such as dark chocolate (in moderation), berries, nuts, and leafy greens.

10. Practice Portion Control: Be mindful of portion sizes to maintain a healthy weight, which can positively impact self-esteem and overall mental health.

11. Eat Regularly: Skipping meals can lead to blood sugar fluctuations, which can affect your mood and energy levels. Aim for regular, balanced meals and snacks throughout the day.

12. Consider Supplements: In some cases, dietary supplements like vitamin D or B vitamins may be recommended by a healthcare professional if you have deficiencies that impact your mental health.

13. Listen to Your Body: Pay attention to how different foods make you feel. Everyone's body responds differently, so it's important to personalize your diet based on your individual needs and sensitivities.

14. Combine Diet with Other Strategies: While diet plays a significant role in mental health, it's just one piece of the puzzle. Combining a mental health diet with regular physical activity, stress management techniques, and seeking support through therapy or counseling can provide a more comprehensive approach to mental well-being.

CHAPTER TWO

14-Day Mental Health Diet Meal Plan

Day 1

- Breakfast: Greek yogurt parfait with mixed berries and a sprinkle of walnuts.
- Lunch: Grilled chicken breast salad with mixed greens, cherry tomatoes, cucumber, and olive oil vinaigrette.
- Snack: Carrot and celery sticks with hummus.
- Dinner: Baked salmon with quinoa and steamed broccoli.

Day 2

- Breakfast: Oatmeal with sliced banana and a teaspoon of almond butter.
- Lunch: Lentil soup with a side of whole-grain bread and a garden salad.
- Snack: Sliced apples with a tablespoon of peanut butter.
- Dinner: Stir-fried tofu with brown rice and mixed vegetables.

Day 3

- Breakfast: Scrambled eggs with spinach and tomatoes.
- Lunch: Chickpea and vegetable curry with a side of brown rice.
- Snack: Greek yogurt with honey and a handful of mixed nuts.
- Dinner: Grilled shrimp with quinoa and roasted asparagus.

Day 4

- Breakfast: Smoothie with spinach, banana, frozen berries, and almond milk.
- Lunch: Turkey and avocado wrap with whole-grain tortilla and a side of mixed greens.
- Snack: Cottage cheese with pineapple chunks.
- Dinner: Baked chicken breast with sweet potato and sautéed spinach.

Day 5

- Breakfast: Whole-grain toast with avocado and poached eggs.
- Lunch: Quinoa salad with chickpeas, bell peppers,

and a lemon-tahini dressing.

- Snack: Sliced cucumbers with tzatziki sauce.

- Dinner: Baked cod with quinoa and roasted Brussels sprouts.

Day 6

- Breakfast: Overnight oats with chia seeds, almond milk, and mixed berries.

- Lunch: Brown rice bowl with grilled tofu, steamed broccoli, and teriyaki sauce.

- Snack: Sliced pears with cottage cheese.

- Dinner: Turkey chili with a side of whole-grain cornbread.

Day 7

- Breakfast: Whole-grain waffles with Greek yogurt and sliced strawberries.

- Lunch: Spinach and feta stuffed chicken breast with quinoa and steamed green beans.

- Snack: Mixed nuts and dried apricots.

- Dinner: Baked salmon with couscous and sautéed spinach.

Day 8

- Breakfast: A smoothie bowl with spinach, banana, mango, and a sprinkle of chia seeds.
- Lunch: Quinoa and black bean salad with diced tomatoes, corn, and a lime-cilantro dressing.
- Snack: Sliced cucumbers with guacamole.
- Dinner: Grilled shrimp skewers with brown rice and steamed broccoli.

Day 9

- Breakfast: Scrambled eggs with diced bell peppers and onions.
- Lunch: Whole-grain pasta with a tomato basil sauce, grilled chicken, and a side of mixed greens.
- Snack: Sliced strawberries with a dollop of Greek yogurt.
- Dinner: Baked cod with quinoa and roasted asparagus.

Day 10

- Breakfast: Whole-grain toast with cottage cheese and sliced peaches.
- Lunch: Turkey and avocado salad with mixed greens

and balsamic vinaigrette.

- Snack: Mixed nuts and dried cranberries.
- Dinner: Baked chicken breast with sweet potato and sautéed spinach.

Day 11

- Breakfast: Oatmeal with sliced banana, a drizzle of honey, and chopped walnuts.
- Lunch: Lentil and vegetable stir-fry with brown rice.
- Snack: Carrot and celery sticks with hummus.
- Dinner: Grilled salmon with quinoa and roasted Brussels sprouts.

Day 12

- Breakfast: Whole-grain waffles with Greek yogurt and mixed berries.
- Lunch: Chickpea and vegetable curry with a side of quinoa.
- Snack: Sliced apples with almond butter.
- Dinner: Baked turkey meatballs with whole-grain spaghetti and a side salad.

Day 13

- Breakfast: Scrambled eggs with spinach and diced tomatoes.
- Lunch: Tofu and vegetable stir-fry with brown rice and a teriyaki glaze.
- Snack: Greek yogurt with honey and a handful of mixed nuts.
- Dinner: Grilled shrimp with quinoa and steamed green beans.

Day 14

- Breakfast: Smoothie with kale, pineapple, banana, and almond milk.
- Lunch: Spinach and feta stuffed chicken breast with quinoa and roasted carrots.
- Snack: Sliced pears with cottage cheese.
- Dinner: Turkey chili with a side of whole-grain cornbread.

CHAPTER THREE

Mental Health Diet Breakfast Recipes

1. Berry and Spinach Smoothie Bowl

Start your day with a burst of vitamins and antioxidants in this vibrant smoothie bowl.

Ingredients:

- 1 cup spinach leaves
- 1/2 cup mixed berries (strawberries, blueberries, raspberries)
- 1 banana
- 1/2 cup Greek yogurt
- 1 tablespoon honey
- 2 tablespoons granola
- Fresh berries and sliced banana for topping

Instructions:

1. Blend spinach, mixed berries, banana, Greek yogurt, and honey until smooth.

2. Pour into a bowl and top with granola, fresh berries, and sliced banana.

3. Enjoy!

Cooking Time: 5 minutes

2. Avocado and Poached Egg Toast

Creamy avocado and perfectly poached eggs make a delicious and nutritious breakfast.

Ingredients:

- 1 ripe avocado
- 2 eggs
- 2 slices whole-grain bread
- Salt and pepper to taste
- Red pepper flakes (optional)
- Fresh cilantro for garnish (optional)

Instructions:

1. Toast the whole-grain bread.

2. Mash the ripe avocado and spread it evenly on the toasted bread.

3. Poach two eggs and place them on top of the avocado.

4. Season with salt, pepper, red pepper flakes (if desired),

and garnish with fresh cilantro.

5. Serve immediately.

Cooking Time: 10 minutes

3. Greek Yogurt Parfait

This Greek yogurt parfait is packed with probiotics, fiber, and antioxidants.

Ingredients:

- 1 cup Greek yogurt
- 1/2 cup granola
- 1/2 cup mixed berries (strawberries, blueberries, raspberries)
- 1 tablespoon honey
- Chopped nuts (e.g., almonds, walnuts) for crunch (optional)

Instructions:

1. Layer Greek yogurt, granola, mixed berries, and honey in a glass or bowl.

2. Repeat the layers.

3. Top with chopped nuts for extra texture.

4. Drizzle with more honey if desired.

5. Enjoy!

Cooking Time: 5 minutes

4. Veggie Omelette

A veggie-packed omelette is a great way to start your day with protein and nutrients.

Ingredients:

- 2 eggs
- 1/4 cup diced bell peppers (any color)
- 1/4 cup diced tomatoes
- 1/4 cup diced onions
- 1/4 cup chopped spinach
- Salt and pepper to taste
- Cooking oil (olive oil or cooking spray)

Instructions:

1. Heat a non-stick skillet over medium-high heat and add a small amount of oil or cooking spray.

2. Whisk the eggs in a bowl and season with salt and pepper.

3. Pour the eggs into the skillet.

4. Sprinkle the diced vegetables evenly over the eggs.

5. Cook until the edges set, then fold the omelette in half.

6. Cook for another minute or two until the eggs are fully set.

7. Slide onto a plate and enjoy!

Cooking Time: 10 minutes

5. Banana and Almond Butter Overnight Oats

These overnight oats are a convenient and nutritious option for busy mornings.

Ingredients:

- 1/2 cup rolled oats
- 1 cup almond milk (or your preferred milk)
- 1 ripe banana, mashed
- 2 tablespoons almond butter
- 1 tablespoon honey (optional)
- Sliced banana and chopped almonds for topping

Instructions:

1. In a jar or container, combine rolled oats, almond milk, mashed banana, almond butter, and honey (if desired).

2. Stir well, cover, and refrigerate overnight.

3. In the morning, give it a good stir, top with sliced banana and chopped almonds.

4. Enjoy your creamy, no-cook breakfast!

Cooking Time: 5 minutes (plus overnight soaking)

6. Spinach and Feta Breakfast Wrap

This savory breakfast wrap is filled with greens and protein to kickstart your day.

Ingredients:

- 2 large eggs
- 1 whole-wheat tortilla
- 1/2 cup fresh spinach leaves
- 2 tablespoons crumbled feta cheese
- Salt and pepper to taste
- Cooking oil (olive oil or cooking spray)

Instructions:

1. In a non-stick skillet over medium heat, sauté the spinach until wilted.

2. Whisk the eggs and pour them into the skillet with the spinach.

3. Cook until the eggs are scrambled.

4. Warm the tortilla in the skillet or microwave.

5. Place the scrambled eggs and feta cheese in the center of the tortilla.

6. Season with salt and pepper.

7. Fold the sides of the tortilla and roll it up.

8. Enjoy your breakfast wrap!

Cooking Time: 10 minutes

7. Peanut Butter and Banana Smoothie

This creamy peanut butter and banana smoothie is both satisfying and nutritious.

Ingredients:

- 1 ripe banana
- 2 tablespoons peanut butter
- 1 cup almond milk (or your preferred milk)
- 1 tablespoon honey (optional)
- Ice cubes (optional)

Instructions:

1. Place the banana, peanut butter, almond milk, and honey (if desired) in a blender.

2. Add ice cubes for a colder and thicker consistency.

3. Blend until smooth.

4. Pour into a glass and enjoy your protein-rich smoothie!

Cooking Time: 5 minutes

8. Chia Seed Pudding

Chia seed pudding is a nutritious and versatile breakfast option that you can customize with various toppings.

Ingredients:

- 3 tablespoons chia seeds
- 1 cup almond milk (or your preferred milk)
- 1 tablespoon honey or maple syrup (optional)
- Fresh fruit (e.g., berries, sliced banana) for topping
- Chopped nuts (e.g., almonds, walnuts) for crunch

Instructions:

1. In a jar or container, combine chia seeds, almond milk, and honey or maple syrup (if desired).

2. Stir well, cover, and refrigerate for at least a few hours or overnight until it thickens.

3. Before serving, top with fresh fruit and chopped nuts.

4. Enjoy your customizable chia seed pudding!

Cooking Time: 5 minutes (plus chilling time)

9. Smoked Salmon and Cream Cheese Bagel

This classic combination of flavors on a whole-grain bagel is a delicious and protein-rich breakfast.

Ingredients:

- 1 whole-grain bagel
- 2 tablespoons light cream cheese
- 2 slices smoked salmon
- Sliced cucumber and red onion for topping
- Fresh dill (optional)
- Lemon wedges (optional)

Instructions:

1. Toast the whole-grain bagel.

2. Spread cream cheese on both bagel halves.

3. Place smoked salmon on one half of the bagel.

4. Top with sliced cucumber, red onion, fresh dill (if desired), and a squeeze of lemon juice (optional).

5. Sandwich the two halves together.

6. Enjoy your satisfying bagel breakfast!

Cooking Time: 5 minutes

10. Blueberry and Almond Oatmeal

A comforting bowl of oatmeal with blueberries and almonds provides fiber, antioxidants, and healthy fats.

Ingredients:

- 1/2 cup rolled oats
- 1 cup water or milk (almond, soy, or your preferred milk)
- 1/2 cup blueberries (fresh or frozen)
- 1 tablespoon almond butter
- 1 tablespoon honey (optional)
- Sliced almonds for topping

Instructions:

1. In a saucepan, bring the water or milk to a boil.

2. Stir in the rolled oats and reduce heat to a simmer.

3. Cook for 5-7 minutes, stirring occasionally, until the oats are creamy.

4. Add blueberries and almond butter, and cook for an additional 2 minutes.

5. Remove from heat, sweeten with honey (if desired), and top with sliced almonds.

6. Enjoy your warm and nourishing oatmeal!

Cooking Time: 10 minutes

Mental Health Diet Lunch Recipes

1. Mediterranean Quinoa Salad

This refreshing salad combines nutrient-rich ingredients for a satisfying and mood-boosting lunch.

Ingredients:

- 1 cup cooked quinoa
- 1 cup cherry tomatoes, halved
- 1 cucumber, diced
- 1/2 cup Kalamata olives, pitted and sliced
- 1/4 cup red onion, finely chopped
- 1/4 cup crumbled feta cheese
- Fresh basil leaves, torn
- Olive oil and balsamic vinegar for dressing
- Salt and pepper to taste

Instructions:

1. In a large bowl, combine quinoa, cherry tomatoes, cucumber, olives, red onion, and feta cheese.

2. Drizzle with olive oil and balsamic vinegar.

3. Season with salt and pepper.

4. Toss gently to combine.

5. Garnish with torn basil leaves.

6. Enjoy your Mediterranean-inspired salad!

Cooking Time: 20 minutes (if quinoa needs to be cooked)

2. Veggie and Hummus Wrap

This veggie-packed wrap with hummus is a quick and nutritious lunch option.

Ingredients:

- 1 whole-wheat tortilla
- 2 tablespoons hummus
- Sliced cucumber, bell peppers, and carrots
- Cherry tomatoes, halved
- Sliced avocado
- Baby spinach leaves
- Feta cheese (optional)
- Salt and pepper to taste

Instructions:

1. Spread hummus evenly on the whole-wheat tortilla.

2. Layer sliced cucumber, bell peppers, carrots, cherry tomatoes, sliced avocado, baby spinach leaves, and feta cheese (if desired).

3. Season with salt and pepper.

4. Roll up the tortilla.

5. Enjoy your easy and nutritious veggie wrap!

Cooking Time: 10 minutes

3. Lentil and Vegetable Soup

A warm bowl of hearty lentil and vegetable soup provides a comforting and nutritious lunch.

Ingredients:

- 1 cup dried green or brown lentils
- 6 cups vegetable broth
- 2 carrots, diced
- 2 celery stalks, diced
- 1 onion, chopped

- 2 cloves garlic, minced

- 1 bay leaf

- 1 teaspoon dried thyme

- Salt and pepper to taste

- Fresh parsley for garnish (optional)

Instructions:

1. Rinse the lentils under cold water and drain.

2. In a large pot, sauté the onion, garlic, carrots, and celery in a bit of olive oil until softened.

3. Add lentils, vegetable broth, bay leaf, and thyme.

4. Bring to a boil, then reduce heat and simmer for 25-30 minutes or until lentils are tender.

5. Season with salt and pepper.

6. Remove the bay leaf.

7. Garnish with fresh parsley if desired.

8. Enjoy your comforting lentil and vegetable soup!

Cooking Time: 45 minutes

4. Spinach and Chickpea Salad with Lemon-Tahini Dressing

This salad is packed with leafy greens, chickpeas, and a zesty lemon-tahini dressing for a satisfying and nutritious lunch.

Ingredients:

- 2 cups fresh spinach leaves
- 1 cup canned chickpeas, drained and rinsed
- 1/4 cup cherry tomatoes, halved
- 1/4 cup cucumber, diced
- 1/4 cup red onion, finely chopped
- 2 tablespoons tahini
- Juice of 1 lemon
- 1 clove garlic, minced
- Salt and pepper to taste
- Chopped fresh mint for garnish (optional)

Instructions:

1. In a large bowl, combine spinach, chickpeas, cherry tomatoes, cucumber, and red onion.

2. In a separate bowl, whisk together tahini, lemon juice,

minced garlic, salt, and pepper.

3. Drizzle the dressing over the salad.

4. Toss gently to coat.

5. Garnish with chopped fresh mint if desired.

6. Enjoy your refreshing spinach and chickpea salad!

Cooking Time: 10 minutes

5. Grilled Chicken and Quinoa Bowl

This protein-packed bowl with grilled chicken and quinoa is both satisfying and nutritious.

Ingredients:

- 1 boneless, skinless chicken breast
- 1 cup cooked quinoa
- 1 cup steamed broccoli florets
- 1/2 cup diced red bell pepper
- 1/4 cup chopped fresh parsley
- 2 tablespoons olive oil
- Juice of 1 lemon
- Salt and pepper to taste

Instructions:

1. Season the chicken breast with salt and pepper.

2. Grill the chicken until cooked through, about 6-8 minutes per side.

3. Slice the grilled chicken into strips.

4. In a bowl, combine cooked quinoa, steamed broccoli, diced red bell pepper, and chopped fresh parsley.

5. Drizzle with olive oil and lemon juice.

6. Season with salt and pepper.

7. Top with sliced grilled chicken.

8. Enjoy your protein-rich quinoa bowl!

Cooking Time: 20 minutes

6. Sweet Potato and Black Bean Salad

This salad combines the natural sweetness of sweet potatoes with protein-rich black beans for a satisfying and nutritious lunch.

Ingredients:

- 2 cups diced sweet potatoes
- 1 can black beans, drained and rinsed
- 1/2 red onion, finely chopped
- 1 red bell pepper, diced
- 1/4 cup chopped cilantro
- Juice of 1 lime
- 2 tablespoons olive oil
- 1 teaspoon cumin
- Salt and pepper to taste

Instructions:

1. Roast the diced sweet potatoes in the oven until tender, about 25-30 minutes at 400°F (200°C).

2. In a large bowl, combine roasted sweet potatoes, black beans, red onion, red bell pepper, and chopped cilantro.

3. In a small bowl, whisk together lime juice, olive oil, cumin, salt, and pepper.

4. Drizzle the dressing over the salad.

5. Toss gently to combine.

6. Enjoy your flavorful sweet potato and black bean salad!

Cooking Time: 35 minutes

7. Tuna and White Bean Salad

This tuna and white bean salad is a protein-rich and satisfying lunch option.

Ingredients:

- 1 can white beans (cannellini or navy), drained and rinsed
- 1 can tuna in water, drained
- 1/4 cup red onion, finely chopped
- 1/4 cup diced celery
- 2 tablespoons chopped fresh parsley
- Juice of 1 lemon
- 2 tablespoons olive oil
- Salt and pepper to taste

Instructions:

1. In a large bowl, combine white beans, tuna, red onion, celery, and chopped fresh parsley.

2. In a small bowl, whisk together lemon juice, olive oil, salt,

and pepper.

3. Drizzle the dressing over the salad.

4. Toss gently to combine.

5. Enjoy your protein-packed tuna and white bean salad!

Cooking Time: 10 minutes

8. Butternut Squash and Chickpea Curry

This butternut squash and chickpea curry is a warm and comforting lunch option with anti-inflammatory properties.

Ingredients:

- 2 cups diced butternut squash
- 1 can chickpeas, drained and rinsed
- 1 onion, chopped
- 2 cloves garlic, minced
- 1 can diced tomatoes
- 1 can coconut milk
- 2 tablespoons curry powder
- Salt and pepper to taste
- Fresh cilantro for garnish (optional)

Instructions:

1. In a large pot, sauté the chopped onion and garlic until fragrant.

2. Add curry powder and cook for another minute.

3. Add diced butternut squash, chickpeas, diced tomatoes, and coconut milk.

4. Season with salt and pepper.

5. Simmer for 20-25 minutes or until the butternut squash is tender.

6. Garnish with fresh cilantro if desired.

7. Enjoy your flavorful butternut squash and chickpea curry!

Cooking Time: 35 minutes

9. Salmon and Asparagus Quinoa Bowl

This quinoa bowl with salmon and asparagus provides omega-3 fatty acids and essential nutrients for a satisfying lunch.

Ingredients:

- 1 salmon fillet
- 1 cup cooked quinoa
- 1 cup steamed asparagus spears
- 1/4 cup sliced cherry tomatoes
- 1/4 cup diced red onion
- 2 tablespoons olive oil
- Juice of 1 lemon
- Salt and pepper to taste

Instructions:

1. Season the salmon fillet with salt and pepper.

2. Grill or bake the salmon until cooked through, about 8-10 minutes.

3. In a bowl, combine cooked quinoa, steamed asparagus, sliced cherry tomatoes, and diced red onion.

4. Drizzle with olive oil and lemon juice.

5. Season with salt and pepper.

6. Top with the grilled salmon.

7. Enjoy your omega-3 rich quinoa bowl!

Cooking Time: 15 minutes

10. Cauliflower and Chickpea Salad with Lemon-Tahini Dressing

This salad features roasted cauliflower and chickpeas with a tangy lemon-tahini dressing for a flavorful and nutritious lunch.

Ingredients:

- 2 cups cauliflower florets
- 1 can chickpeas, drained and rinsed
- 1/4 cup red bell pepper, diced
- 1/4 cup cucumber, diced
- 2 tablespoons tahini
- Juice of 1 lemon
- 1 clove garlic, minced
- Salt and pepper to taste
- Chopped fresh parsley for garnish (optional)

Instructions:

1. Toss cauliflower florets and chickpeas with olive oil, salt,

and pepper.

2. Roast in the oven at 425°F (220°C) for 20-25 minutes or until cauliflower is tender and slightly crispy.

3. In a large bowl, combine roasted cauliflower and chickpeas with diced red bell pepper and cucumber.

4. In a separate bowl, whisk together tahini, lemon juice, minced garlic, salt, and pepper.

5. Drizzle the dressing over the salad.

6. Toss gently to combine.

7. Garnish with chopped fresh parsley if desired.

8. Enjoy your flavorful cauliflower and chickpea salad!

Cooking Time: 35 minutes

CHAPTER FOUR

Mental Health Diet Dinner Recipes

1. Baked Salmon with Lemon-Dill Sauce

This baked salmon with a zesty lemon-dill sauce is rich in omega-3 fatty acids, which are beneficial for mental health.

Ingredients:

- 2 salmon fillets
- 2 tablespoons olive oil
- Juice of 1 lemon
- 2 cloves garlic, minced
- 1 tablespoon fresh dill, chopped
- Salt and pepper to taste
- Lemon slices for garnish (optional)

Instructions:

1. Preheat the oven to 375°F (190°C).

2. Place salmon fillets on a baking sheet.

3. In a bowl, whisk together olive oil, lemon juice, minced garlic, chopped dill, salt, and pepper.

4. Drizzle the mixture over the salmon.

5. Bake for 12-15 minutes or until salmon flakes easily with a fork.

6. Garnish with lemon slices if desired.

7. Enjoy your omega-3 rich baked salmon!

Cooking Time: 15 minutes

2. Quinoa-Stuffed Bell Peppers

These quinoa-stuffed bell peppers are packed with protein and nutrients for a wholesome dinner.

Ingredients:

- 4 bell peppers, any color
- 1 cup cooked quinoa
- 1 can black beans, drained and rinsed
- 1 cup diced tomatoes
- 1 cup corn kernels (fresh or frozen)
- 1/2 cup diced red onion
- 1 teaspoon chili powder
- Salt and pepper to taste
- Grated cheese for topping (optional)

Instructions:

1. Preheat the oven to 375°F (190°C).

2. Cut the tops off the bell peppers and remove the seeds.

3. In a bowl, combine cooked quinoa, black beans, diced tomatoes, corn kernels, diced red onion, chili powder, salt, and pepper.

4. Stuff each bell pepper with the quinoa mixture.

5. Place the stuffed bell peppers in a baking dish.

6. Cover with foil and bake for 25-30 minutes.

7. If using cheese, remove the foil, sprinkle with grated cheese, and bake for an additional 5 minutes until cheese is melted and bubbly.

8. Enjoy your hearty quinoa-stuffed bell peppers!

Cooking Time: 35 minutes

3. Lemon Garlic Shrimp Pasta

This lemon garlic shrimp pasta is a flavorful and easy-to-make dinner option.

Ingredients:

- 8 oz whole-grain pasta
- 1 lb large shrimp, peeled and deveined
- 2 tablespoons olive oil
- 4 cloves garlic, minced
- Juice and zest of 1 lemon
- 1/4 cup fresh parsley, chopped
- Red pepper flakes (optional)
- Salt and pepper to taste
- Grated Parmesan cheese for topping (optional)

Instructions:

1. Cook the pasta according to package instructions until al dente. Drain and set aside.

2. In a large skillet, heat olive oil over medium-high heat.

3. Add minced garlic and sauté for about 1 minute until fragrant.

4. Add the shrimp and cook for 2-3 minutes on each side until they turn pink and opaque.

5. Stir in lemon juice, lemon zest, chopped parsley, red

pepper flakes (if desired), salt, and pepper.

6. Add the cooked pasta to the skillet and toss to combine.

7. If using, sprinkle with grated Parmesan cheese.

8. Enjoy your lemon garlic shrimp pasta!

Cooking Time: 20 minutes

4. Vegan Lentil and Vegetable Stir-Fry

This vegan lentil and vegetable stir-fry is packed with plant-based protein and colorful veggies.

Ingredients:

- 1 cup dried green or brown lentils
- 2 cups vegetable broth
- 1 tablespoon olive oil
- 1 onion, chopped
- 2 cloves garlic, minced
- 2 cups mixed vegetables (e.g., bell peppers, broccoli, snap peas)
- 1/4 cup low-sodium soy sauce or tamari
- 1 tablespoon cornstarch (optional for thicker sauce)
- Cooked brown rice for serving

Instructions:

1. Rinse the lentils under cold water and drain.

2. In a saucepan, combine lentils and vegetable broth.

3. Bring to a boil, then reduce heat and simmer for 25-30 minutes or until lentils are tender.

4. In a large skillet, heat olive oil over medium-high heat.

5. Add chopped onion and minced garlic, and sauté until softened.

6. Add mixed vegetables and stir-fry for about 5 minutes until they are tender-crisp.

7. In a small bowl, whisk together soy sauce and cornstarch (if using).

8. Pour the sauce over the vegetable mixture and stir to combine.

9. Add the cooked lentils and toss to combine.

10. Serve over cooked brown rice.

11. Enjoy your vegan lentil and vegetable stir-fry!

Cooking Time: 45 minutes

5. Roasted Chicken and Vegetables

This simple and wholesome dinner features roasted chicken and a medley of colorful vegetables.

Ingredients:

- 4 bone-in, skin-on chicken thighs
- 2 cups mixed vegetables (e.g., carrots, potatoes, bell peppers)
- 2 tablespoons olive oil
- 2 cloves garlic, minced
- 1 teaspoon dried thyme
- Salt and pepper to taste
- Fresh herbs (e.g., rosemary, parsley) for garnish (optional)

Instructions:

1. Preheat the oven to 425°F (220°C).

2. In a large baking dish, combine chicken thighs and mixed vegetables.

3. Drizzle with olive oil and sprinkle minced garlic, dried

thyme, salt, and pepper over the chicken and vegetables.

4. Toss everything to coat evenly.

5. Roast in the oven for 35-40 minutes or until the chicken is cooked through and the vegetables are tender.

6. Garnish with fresh herbs if desired.

7. Enjoy your simple and satisfying roasted chicken and

Cooking Time: 45 minutes

6. Sweet Potato and Black Bean Tacos

These sweet potato and black bean tacos are a flavorful and nutritious dinner option.

Ingredients:

- 2 medium sweet potatoes, peeled and diced
- 1 can black beans, drained and rinsed
- 1 teaspoon chili powder
- 1/2 teaspoon cumin
- Salt and pepper to taste
- 8 small whole-wheat tortillas
- Sliced avocado, salsa, and fresh cilantro for topping

(optional)

Instructions:

1. Preheat the oven to 400°F (200°C).

2. Toss sweet potato cubes with chili powder, cumin, salt, and pepper.

3. Roast in the oven for 20-25 minutes or until tender and slightly crispy.

4. In a saucepan, heat black beans over medium heat and season with salt and pepper.

5. Warm the whole-wheat tortillas.

6. Assemble the tacos by layering roasted sweet potatoes, black beans, sliced avocado, salsa, and fresh cilantro.

7. Enjoy your sweet potato and black bean tacos!

Cooking Time: 30 minutes

7. Broccoli and Mushroom Quinoa Bowl

This quinoa bowl with broccoli and mushrooms is a nutritious and satisfying dinner choice.

Ingredients:

- 1 cup cooked quinoa
- 2 cups broccoli florets
- 1 cup sliced mushrooms
- 2 cloves garlic, minced
- 2 tablespoons olive oil
- 1 tablespoon low-sodium soy sauce or tamari
- Salt and pepper to taste
- Sliced green onions and sesame seeds for garnish (optional)

Instructions:

1. Steam or blanch the broccoli florets until tender-crisp.

2. In a large skillet, heat olive oil over medium-high heat.

3. Add minced garlic and sauté until fragrant.

4. Add sliced mushrooms and sauté until they release their moisture and turn golden.

5. Add cooked quinoa and broccoli to the skillet.

6. Drizzle with soy sauce, and season with salt and pepper.

7. Toss everything to combine.

8. Garnish with sliced green onions and sesame seeds if desired.

9. Enjoy your broccoli and mushroom quinoa bowl!

Cooking Time: 20 minutes

8. Spaghetti Squash with Pesto and Cherry Tomatoes

This spaghetti squash dish with homemade pesto and cherry tomatoes is a light and flavorful dinner option.

Ingredients:

- 1 spaghetti squash
- 1 cup cherry tomatoes, halved
- Grated Parmesan cheese for topping (optional)

For Pesto:

- 2 cups fresh basil leaves
- 1/4 cup pine nuts
- 1/4 cup grated Parmesan cheese
- 2 cloves garlic

- Juice of 1 lemon

- 1/4 cup olive oil

- Salt and pepper to taste

Instructions:

1. Preheat the oven to 375°F (190°C).

2. Cut the spaghetti squash in half lengthwise, scoop out the seeds, and place it cut side down on a baking sheet.

3. Bake for 35-45 minutes until the squash is tender and the flesh shreds easily with a fork.

4. While the squash is roasting, prepare the pesto by blending basil, pine nuts, grated Parmesan cheese, garlic, lemon juice, olive oil, salt, and pepper in a food processor until smooth.

5. Scrape the cooked spaghetti squash flesh into a bowl, and toss with pesto and halved cherry tomatoes.

6. If desired, sprinkle with grated Parmesan cheese.

7. Enjoy your spaghetti squash with pesto and cherry tomatoes!

Cooking Time: 45 minutes

9. Vegan Chickpea and Vegetable Curry

This vegan chickpea and vegetable curry is a flavorful and satisfying dinner option with anti-inflammatory properties.

Ingredients:

- 2 cups cauliflower florets
- 1 can chickpeas, drained and rinsed
- 1 cup diced carrots
- 1 cup diced potatoes
- 1 onion, chopped
- 2 cloves garlic, minced
- 1 can diced tomatoes
- 1 can coconut milk
- 2 tablespoons curry powder
- Salt and pepper to taste
- Fresh cilantro for garnish (optional)

Instructions:

1. In a large pot, sauté chopped onion and minced garlic until softened.

2. Add curry powder and cook for another minute.

3. Add cauliflower florets, chickpeas, diced carrots, diced potatoes, diced tomatoes, and coconut milk.

4. Season with salt and pepper.

5. Simmer for 20-25 minutes or until the vegetables are tender.

6. Garnish with fresh cilantro if desired.

7. Enjoy your flavorful vegan chickpea and vegetable curry!

Cooking Time: 45 minutes

10. Teriyaki Tofu Stir-Fry

This teriyaki tofu stir-fry is a delicious and protein-rich dinner option.

Ingredients:

- 1 block firm tofu, cubed
- 2 cups mixed vegetables (e.g., bell peppers, broccoli, snap peas)
- 1/4 cup low-sodium teriyaki sauce
- 2 tablespoons olive oil
- Cooked brown rice or quinoa for serving

Instructions:

1. Press the tofu to remove excess moisture, then cube it.

2. Heat olive oil in a large skillet over medium-high heat.

3. Add tofu cubes and cook until they turn golden brown on all sides.

4. Remove tofu from the skillet and set aside.

5. In the same skillet, add mixed vegetables and stir-fry until tender-crisp.

6. Return tofu to the skillet, add teriyaki sauce, and stir to combine.

7. Serve over cooked brown rice or quinoa.

8. Enjoy your teriyaki tofu stir-fry!

Cooking Time: 30 minutes

Mental Health Diet Snacks Recipes

1. Greek Yogurt and Berry Parfait

This Greek yogurt and berry parfait is a protein-packed and antioxidant-rich snack to keep you energized and satisfied.

Ingredients:

- 1 cup Greek yogurt
- 1/2 cup mixed berries (strawberries, blueberries, raspberries)
- 1 tablespoon honey (optional)
- Granola for topping (optional)

Instructions:

1. In a glass or bowl, layer Greek yogurt and mixed berries.

2. Drizzle with honey if desired.

3. Top with granola for added crunch.

4. Enjoy your creamy and fruity parfait!

Preparation Time: 5 minutes

2. Almond Butter and Banana Rice Cakes

These almond butter and banana rice cakes are a quick and satisfying snack with healthy fats and potassium.

Ingredients:

- Rice cakes

- Almond butter

- Sliced banana

- Honey (optional)

- Chia seeds for topping (optional)

Instructions:

1. Spread almond butter on rice cakes.

2. Top with sliced banana.

3. Drizzle with honey if desired.

4. Sprinkle with chia seeds for added nutrition.

5. Enjoy your crunchy and creamy rice cake snack!

Preparation Time: 5 minutes

3. Hummus and Veggie Sticks

Hummus and veggie sticks are a nutritious and fiber-rich snack that's perfect for dipping.

Ingredients:

- Baby carrots

- Cucumber sticks

- Bell pepper strips

- Cherry tomatoes

- Snap peas

- Hummus for dipping

Instructions:

1. Wash and chop the veggies into sticks or strips.

2. Serve with a side of hummus for dipping.

3. Enjoy your crunchy and colorful veggie snack!

Preparation Time: 10 minutes

4. Baked Sweet Potato Chips

These baked sweet potato chips are a healthier alternative to store-bought chips, rich in vitamins and fiber.

Ingredients:

- 2 medium sweet potatoes

- Olive oil

- Salt and paprika for seasoning (optional)

Instructions:

1. Preheat the oven to 375°F (190°C).

2. Slice sweet potatoes thinly using a mandoline or a sharp knife.

3. Toss the slices in a bowl with a drizzle of olive oil.

4. Arrange the slices on a baking sheet in a single layer.

5. Season with salt and paprika (if desired).

6. Bake for 20-25 minutes or until crisp, flipping them halfway.

7. Allow to cool before enjoying your homemade sweet potato chips!

Preparation Time: 35 minutes

5. Avocado and Tomato Salsa

Avocado and tomato salsa is a creamy and nutritious dip for whole-grain crackers or vegetable sticks.

Ingredients:

- 2 ripe avocados
- 2 tomatoes, diced
- 1/4 red onion, finely chopped

- 1/4 cup cilantro, chopped

- Juice of 1 lime

- Salt and pepper to taste

Instructions:

1. Mash the avocados in a bowl.

2. Add diced tomatoes, chopped red onion, cilantro, and lime juice.

3. Season with salt and pepper.

4. Mix until well combined.

5. Serve with whole-grain crackers or vegetable sticks.

6. Enjoy your creamy avocado salsa!

Preparation Time: 10 minutes

6. Trail Mix

Trail mix is a versatile and nutrient-packed snack that you can customize with your favorite nuts, seeds, and dried fruits.

Ingredients:

- Almonds

- Walnuts

- Pumpkin seeds

- Dried cranberries

- Dried apricots, chopped

- Dark chocolate chips (optional)

Instructions:

1. Combine all ingredients in a bowl in your desired quantities.

2. Toss to mix.

3. Portion into snack-sized bags for easy grab-and-go options.

4. Enjoy your energizing trail mix!

Preparation Time: 5 minutes

7. Cucumber and Hummus Bites

Cucumber and hummus bites are a refreshing and low-calorie snack that's perfect for a quick pick-me-up.

Ingredients:

- Cucumber slices

- Hummus

- Cherry tomatoes (optional)

Instructions:

1. Slice the cucumber into rounds.

2. Spread a small dollop of hummus on each cucumber slice.

3. If desired, top with a cherry tomato half.

4. Enjoy your crisp and creamy cucumber bites!

Preparation Time: 5 minutes

8. Chia Seed Pudding with Berries

Chia seed pudding with berries is a fiber-rich and omega-3 packed snack that's both satisfying and nutritious.

Ingredients:

- 3 tablespoons chia seeds
- 1 cup almond milk (or your preferred milk)
- 1/2 teaspoon vanilla extract
- Mixed berries (strawberries, blueberries, raspberries)
- Honey (optional)

Instructions:

1. In a jar or container, combine chia seeds, almond milk,

and vanilla extract.

2. Stir well, cover, and refrigerate for at least a few hours or overnight until it thickens.

3. Before serving, top with mixed berries and drizzle with honey if desired.

4. Enjoy your customizable chia seed pudding!

Preparation Time: 5 minutes (plus chilling time)

9. Cottage Cheese and Pineapple

Cottage cheese and pineapple is a simple and protein-rich snack with a sweet and tangy twist.

Ingredients:

- Cottage cheese
- Fresh pineapple chunks

Instructions:

1. Place a scoop of cottage cheese in a bowl.

2. Top with fresh pineapple chunks.

3. Enjoy your creamy and tropical snack!

Preparation Time: 5 minutes

10. Roasted Edamame

Roasted edamame is a crunchy and protein-packed snack that's perfect for satisfying your savory cravings.

Ingredients:

- Frozen edamame, thawed
- Olive oil
- Seasonings (e.g., sea salt, garlic powder, smoked paprika)

Instructions:

1. Preheat the oven to 375°F (190°C).

2. Toss thawed edamame in a bowl with a drizzle of olive oil and your choice of seasonings.

3. Spread edamame on a baking sheet in a single layer.

4. Roast for 15-20 minutes until crispy, shaking the pan occasionally.

5. Allow to cool before enjoying your roasted edamame!

CONCLUSION

In conclusion, a mental health diet is not just a concept; it's a powerful and holistic approach to nourishing both the body and the mind. Throughout this exploration of dietary choices and their impact on mental well-being, it has become clear that what we eat plays a pivotal role in shaping our mental health.

The brain, like any other organ, requires proper nutrients to function optimally, and a balanced diet can significantly influence mood, cognition, and emotional stability.

A mental health diet prioritizes nutrient-dense foods rich in vitamins, minerals, antioxidants, and essential fatty acids. Such a diet encompasses a wide variety of whole foods, including fruits, vegetables, lean proteins, whole grains, nuts, seeds, and legumes.

These foods provide the building blocks for neurotransmitters, the chemical messengers of the brain, and support the body's natural defenses against oxidative stress and inflammation, which are linked to mental health disorders.

In addition to the physical benefits, a mental health diet can foster a positive relationship with food and eating. It encourages mindful consumption and an awareness of the body's hunger and fullness cues, promoting a healthier attitude toward eating. Furthermore, it discourages excessive intake of highly processed, sugary, and fatty foods that can contribute to mood swings and energy crashes.

A mental health diet should be viewed as one component of a comprehensive approach to mental wellness. It works in synergy with other aspects, such as regular physical activity, stress management, quality sleep, and social connections.

Ultimately, making dietary choices that prioritize mental health can be a transformative and empowering journey. It offers individuals the opportunity to take an active role in their well-being and enhance their quality of life. Consulting with healthcare professionals or registered dietitians can provide personalized guidance in crafting a mental health diet tailored to individual needs and goals.

By embracing a balanced and nourishing diet, individuals can take a significant step toward achieving better mental health and a more vibrant and fulfilling life.

www.ingramcontent.com/pod-product-compliance
Lightning Source LLC
Chambersburg PA
CBHW071052260726
48661CB00006B/2243